In the *Cradle* of *Love*

DUAA ALI WARSI

Dedication

*The purpose behind writing this book is
my universe—the woman who brought me into this world,
my best friend, my secret keeper—my Maa.
I have tried my best to convey how much
I love and admire this graceful woman,
but I know that words will never truly do her justice.
No matter how hard I try, I'll always fall short of
capturing the depth of my love for her.*
Happy Birthday!!

CONTENTS

ABOUT THE AUTHOR

Duaa Ali Warsi was born in 1999 in Karachi, Pakistan. She grew up and finished her studies there, earning her bachelor's degree before moving to Dubai to pursue her master's. With an ENTJ personality, Duaa is ambitious and full of ideas, though not everyone quite understands her perspective. During her job search, one of her mentors, someone she deeply admired, pointed out that she had an ENTJ personality. It was a revelation that helped her understand herself better. She cherishes her alone time, often retreating to her own little world where she can focus on the things she loves.

She is passionate about painting, capturing her thoughts and emotions on canvas. Now, Duaa is on a path to becoming a filmmaker, pouring her passion and creativity into a craft that allows her to tell stories that resonate deeply. Whether it's through painting, filming moments, or immersing herself in her love for cars, Duaa finds inspiration in everything around her. But what excites her most is traveling, exploring new places, meeting new people, and embracing the unknown with open arms.

CHAPTER 1

THE NIGHT SHE BECAME MORE

The wind was brisk and chill, with a soft frostiness under the oblivious moonbeam. Streetlights put a golden blush on the streets, their beams bending through icy fog in the air. It was the holy month of Ramadan, and the night pulse was exceptional. The sky was a deep canvas dotted with stars that seemed clearer and sharper against the cold of winter. The windowpanes, with the illumination of the lamp, shone moderately. After Iftar meals, the roads came alive with people visiting the mosque for Taraweeh prayers.

She was a visual sensation like adolescence; her eyes were midnight twin pools, enormous and twinkling like the heavens had dispersed their stars within. Her warm, dark brown eyes seemed to hold a quiet universe like there was always more to her than what you saw at first glance. Her long, glossy black hair surrounded her face, falling effortlessly in soft waves that caught the light. It wasn't just picturesque; it reflected her young-at-heart energy, radiant and full of life.

At 18, she was striding onto a stage she hadn't planned for. She was pregnant with her first child, a little life due to arrive in January. The thought of turning into a mother was both exciting and overwhelming. She felt a combination of sentiments every day, an instant of enthusiasm at the thought of holding her baby stable with the terror of all the unknowns onward. Even as she experienced this astonishing journey, there was quiet vigor in her. She didn't have all the solutions, but she was ready to take it one step at a time, understanding that life would be improved indefinitely.

She was occupied in the kitchen, the calm pulse of her work sustaining her when an abrupt, intense pain made her halt. She leaned on the counter, clinging to it rigidly as her heart began to race. Something was happening, something she wasn't anticipating.

Her family momentarily leaped into action, helping her into the vehicle. The drive to the hospital felt bizarre. The serene winter paths clouded past, but inside the car, everything felt vital and anxious. She hadn't been ready for this—not yet. Her baby wasn't expected to arrive until January.

The insight began to sink in when they reached the hospital. The staff verified it was in labor. Fright and pleasure whirled together, her thoughts rushing as she tried to process it all. She was about to have her baby, weeks ahead of the time she'd prepared.

The night felt eternal, every moment yielding into the next. But as the first daylight of Sunday morning edged in, everything shifted. The room was packed with the exceptional sound of her baby's first cry. Tears flooded down her face as they laid her offspring in her arms, bundled in a soft layer.

Staring down at her baby girl's little, perfect face, she felt an overwhelming impulse of love and admiration. In that split second, nothing else was significant. All the anxiety and hesitation disappeared, leaving only her and her daughter together at the beginning of something new and extraordinary.

CHAPTER 2

SONGS OF COMFORT, SOUNDS OF JOY

The connection between a new mum and a daughter is something words can hardly describe. It's tender, natural, and life-changing in ways she never anticipated. From the very first moment she holds her baby in her shuddering arms, something clicks. It's as though an unseen string binds them together, growing stronger with every passing second.

The early days are a haze of sleepless nights and frequent care. Fatigued but firm, she hums soft cradle songs, her voice just more than a whisper. Those tunes are as much for her infant as they are for herself—a way to calm the baby in her arms and repeat to herself that she's sufficient. The baby, so tiny and helpless, notices protection in touch, her heartbeat, her aura. For those first few weeks, she's the whole world.

Then come the smirks. The first one feels magical, fading away the tiredness and bringing tears of joy to her eyes. Soon, the quiet flashes of songs are changed by tiny bursts of laughter, the kind of unfiltered bliss only a baby can have. And before she knows it, she's laughing too—real, free laughter that she didn't recognize she'd been missing.

The connection becomes deep in these small moments—feeding her baby, gently bathing her, or simply watching her sleep. It's a connection built on trust: the baby depends on her for everything, and the mother acquires a power she didn't know she had.

Every day, the tempo of their lives combines calm lullabies and happy chuckles. Those twinkling of relaxation and joy smooth out their world, forming a relationship that will drive them through the years ahead. It's not ideal and not always easy, but it's theirs—and it's everything.

After spending a week in the hospital, she finally came home with her little one, and her home was filled with love and laughter. Mehnaz was fond of writing. She decided to write and dedicate a poem to her baby to express her love for her baby. Though she was busy the whole day, she managed to take some time out to write at night when her baby was sleeping. She was so excited to write that she finished writing within a few days and published it in a newspaper to tell the world how blessed she was.

From the moment her baby arrived in the world, the mother's life completely changed. Her own desires, formerly at the lead, became a second thought. Every bit of strength, every minute of her day, orbited her newborn.

Even when she was tired, she stayed up through the night, swaying her baby in her arms or softly patting her back, her weary eyes watching the tiny chest rise and fall as the baby slept calmly. If sleep came at all, it was in stolen minutes, but she didn't care—her baby's relief counted more than her own.

When she felt sick and tired, she shrugged it off. There was no time to think about herself, no time to relax. Her baby's sobs were her only worry, and she pushed through her own distress to ensure her little one was fed, warm, and content. To her, being a mum meant putting her baby's needs above everything, even her own well-being.

The thought of her baby falling ill was intolerable. She eyed her like a hawk, clearing her tiny hands and face, keeping her bundled up against the common cold, and guaranteeing her atmosphere was clean and safe. Every sniff or slight fever was met with instant action: an appointment with the doctor, soothing medications, or sleepless nights spent by the crib, keeping watch.

Her love was profound and all-encompassing. She wanted nothing more than to keep her baby healthy, happy, and protected from hurt. Every sacrifice felt small in contrast to the joy of seeing her baby beam and the peace of mind of knowing her little one was flourishing. For her, parenthood wasn't just a role—it was her whole being, her determination, her greatest reward.

CHAPTER 3

TINY STEPS

The day her baby started crawling was a moment she would never forget. It began like any other day, with her little one playing on the gentle mat she had delicately placed out. The clothes were drying in the sun, hanging on the wire. She went out on the terrace to bring the clothes. As she entered her room, she saw Anna crawling and struggling to get to her toy, which was a bit out of reach. Mehnaz smiled and started folding clothes nearby, glancing over every few seconds to check on her baby. Then, something changed; her baby inclined forward, her tiny hands pushing against the floor, and with shaky willpower, she moved.

Mehnaz stopped for a moment, her heart missing a beat. "Did she just crawl?" she murmured, her voice scarcely noticeable. Her baby attempted again, this time scooting forward a few more inches. An expression of amusement bolted across the mother's lips, tears welling up in her eyes as delight and pleasure submerged her heart.

She dropped everything and fell onto the ground, applauding her little one. "Come on, baby! You can do it!" she said, her voice full of praise. Anna looked up at her, chuckled, and attempted again, moving wobblingly but firmly across the rug.

Mehnaz couldn't stop smiling. She gave a round of applause, her enthusiasm spreading over, and called for her family to come and witness. "She's crawling!" she declared, her voice full of amazement.

Watching her baby develop and achieve this milestone was sentimental. She felt a tremendous sense of joy in her little one's progress and a twinge of nostalgia for how swiftly time passed. It felt like she was rocking her newborn in her arms just yesterday, and now she was moving across the floor with growing certainty.

That night, as she put her baby into bed, she couldn't stop rerunning the moment in her mind. Her heart was full, and she murmured softly, "You're growing so quickly, my little one. I'm so proud of you." It may be an insignificant step for her baby, but for Mehnaz, it was a massive hop in the tremendous journey of seeing her child grow.

She hadn't anticipated it happening that day; it was just another ordinary winter afternoon in 1999. She wanted to capture the moment, to save it forever, but this was 1999—there were no smartphones in her pocket, no direct way to record it. She didn't even have a camcorder at the time. She experienced a wrench of distress that she couldn't save this breakthrough in a video to watch time after time. But at that instant, it didn't matter. What she did have was vivid and vibrant remembrance, carved into her heart like a valued picture.

Just months ago, she had been holding a little, dependent newborn in her arms, and now, here she was, crawling across the floor, one step closer to an independent lifestyle.

Even without a video recording, the memory stayed with her. She knew she would hold it forever—her baby's first crawl, her happiness and joy, and the tremendous pride of watching her little one grow before her eyes.

CHAPTER 4

IN SAFE ARMS

Anna was the first child born into the family after many years, which made her arrival even more exceptional. Everyone admired her, and it appeared as if she never spent a moment alone in her crib. Her kind family, including her young uncles and aunts, couldn't get enough of her.

Mehnaz, Anna's mother, had wed at 18 and brought Anna into this world a year later. As the first among her siblings, Mehnaz's baby gave the family a new ripple of happiness and enjoyment. Everyone adored Anna, willing to shower her with love and attention.

It became a daily routine for the family to take turns holding her in their arms, but it wasn't always calm. Teasing arguments would break out over whose chance it was. "You've been holding her forever; now it's my turn!" they would say, smiling.

Even after a long day at work, Anna's uncle would come home exhausted but light up at the glimpse of her. He would hurry to hold her, all his tiredness gone. Whenever anyone in the family walked out, even just to the corner shop, they'd insist on taking Anna along. She became a part of every day out, big or small. If acquaintances came over, they'd proudly bring Anna out, eager to introduce her and show off her bright smile and curious eyes.

Anna was the core of the family, the center of their world. Her existence brought everyone closer together, filling the house with glee, tenderness, and pleasure. She wasn't just a baby; she was the family's shared treasure, cherished by all.

Anna was not just the center of attention; she was extremely protected, specifically by her mother. From the start, Mehnaz clarified that Anna's well-being came above everything else. If anyone, even inadvertently, did something that might hurt Anna or distress her, Mehnaz didn't delay stepping in. She would confront anyone—whether it was a family member or a guest—who she felt wasn't being careful enough.

"Be gentle with her!" she'd say confidently, her voice containing both love and power. Even if someone accidentally raised their tone near Anna, Mehnaz would immediately step in, her defensive abilities kicking in. Nobody in the family risked speaking bitterly to Anna or shouting in any way that might disturb her.

Mehnaz wasn't terrified to disagree if it meant keeping Anna safe. If someone suggested something she felt wasn't pleasant for her offspring, she would voice her opinion, explaining why it wasn't suitable.

The family swiftly discovered that Anna was forbidden from any comments or harsh words. If Anna cried or seemed troubled, Mehnaz would instantly rush to her, holding her in her arms and muttering calming words until she pacified down.

To Mehnaz, her love wasn't just a sentiment; it was an obligation, a passion, and the very core of her being. Her family came to understand that a mother's love is not something to take lightly. It's a strength that structures life, shields purity, and develops a child's nature in ways nothing else can.

In her firm devotion to Anna, Mehnaz showed everyone around her that a mother's love is unmatched—something to be respected, admired, and appreciated above all else. It's not just love; it's a lifespan of providing, shielding, and putting her child before herself, no matter what.

CHAPTER 5

WINDS OF CHANGE

The TV lounge was alive with enthusiasm, a radiant blend of colors and glee soaking the air. A year had passed since Anna was born, and the family decided to celebrate her first birthday with as much passion and joy as they could gather. The walls were decorated with helium balloons in every color possible, staggering lightly with each air breeze. Glowing candles covered the room, their warm light adding a mystic touch to the cheerful environment.

Her aunt had spent the entire day baking a cake that was as astonishing as it was delicious. It stood pompously on the table, covered with detailed swirls of icing and a single cake candle waiting to be ignited. Her uncles, always the center of any crowd, had taken control of snacks and party poppers. They had gone out of their way to find the most colorful poppers they could, eager to see Anna's reaction when the confetti blasted into the air.

Mehnaz and her husband had spent the week preparing every part. From welcoming friends and family to selecting the perfect gifts and clothes for their daughter, they had poured their hearts into making the day exceptional. Anna's father had even insisted on choosing a tiny crown for her, believing she was worthy of nothing less than looking like the duchess she was to him.

As the evening loomed, the house became energetic with the coming of people. Anna, dressed in a frilly white and black dress and her tiny tiara, sat in her mother's arms, her eclectic eyes taking in the astounding view around her.

When it was time for the cake, everyone grouped around, their tones merging into a symphonic choir of "Happy Birthday." Anna's small hands moved out, intrigued by the flaming candle before her. With the assistance of her parents, she succeeded in blowing it out, her chuckles initiating an outburst of clapping. Her uncles, true to their scheme, exploded the confetti, launching a shower of colors into the air that left Anna screaming with joy.

The rest of the late evening was filled with laughter and love. Her grandparents shared tales of her first year, recounting achievements and moments that had brought so much pleasure to the family. Presents were opened, each one met with enthusiasm and gratefulness, even if Anna was more fascinated by the scrunching gift-wrapping paper than the gifts themselves.

As the party ended and the guests started to leave, Mehnaz realized she was holding Anna close, observing her tiny head resting against her shoulder. In that moment, as she held her daughter close, she felt a deep sense of gratitude—for Anna, for her family, and for the love that bound them all together, stronger than ever.

A year had passed, and with it came the winds of change. Anna was growing, her aura changing their lives in ways they could never have envisioned.

CHAPTER 6

ANNA'S FIRST STEPS WITH A FEATHERED FRIEND

On a hazy morning, Anna's grandma was in the kitchen, peeling fruits and making a fruit container. Anna sat near her on the floor, surrounded by her chosen toys, happily chatting to herself.

In their home, they had an energetic parrot who was hardly caged, free to wander wherever it wanted. But Anna had always been a little cautious of the bird, her tiny heart missing a beat whenever it got too close. That morning, the parrot rested easily on top of the fridge, its clear eyes inspecting the room.

Without threat, the bird flapped its wings and settled near Anna, frightening her. Wide-eyed and suspicious, Anna screamed and, in an unexpected rush of willpower, pushed herself up and ran away in her woozy, unstable way.

Grandma, silently viewing the scene, couldn't help but smile. "Look at her!" she called out, her tone full of happiness as she turned toward the corridor. "The parrot made her stroll! And here we've all been trying for weeks to get her to take her first steps."

Her glee rippled through the house, capturing everyone's attention. As they watched Anna's tiny feet shuffle across the floor, they were filled with amusement and began to cheer. Unaware of its new role as Anna's accidental instructor, the parrot returned to its perch, shrieking happily as if to join in the celebration.

That day, the family celebrated Anna's first walk and the surprising way they had come about – a little help from a feathered friend.

CHAPTER 7

THE FIRST DISTANCE

It was a windy morning that appeared to hint at change. For Anna and her family, it was no usual day, it was her first day of school, a pioneering event that filled the atmosphere with enthusiasm and a bit of apprehension.

Anna's parents had spent weeks visiting schools, cautiously contemplating which one would be the finest fit for their little munchkin. After evaluating all the choices, they opted for a nearby school that would simplify Mehnaz's everyday routine. The choice wasn't just feasible; it came with optimism. They trusted that being around kids her age would aid Anna in starting to talk. She was only 1.5 years old, and though she spoke in her gentle ways, they were willing to hear her voice form into language.

The arrangements felt almost ritualistic. Mehnaz and her husband took Anna shopping, selecting everything she needed. Her small yellow duck-shaped bag was their desired find, complete with a lunchbox and water bottle. Her brisk and newly ironed uniform was carefully folded in its bag, prepared for the big day. And then there were the shoes—small, extremely cute, and just the right fit for her small feet.

That morning, the house hummed with energy. Mehnaz clothed Anna with care, fastening the buttons of her uniform and fixing her hair into two ponies. Anna, as always, was interested in everything, her wide eyes ensuing every move her mother made. When she was completely ready, standing there in her tiny shoes, Mehnaz couldn't help but stop. Her little girl looked so grown up and yet so little.

The walk to school felt longer than usual. Anna gripped her new bag, its straps almost too large for her tiny fingers. Mehnaz held her hand for most of the way, cherishing these last moments of closeness before the school day commenced. She snuck glances at Anna, remembering how her pigtails swayed with every step and how her little face lit up when she noticed interesting things along the road.

At the school gate, realism sets in. The teacher beamed warmly as Mehnaz handed Anna over, her tiny hand gliding from her mother's grip. Mehnaz's heart tightened as she saw her daughter disappear into an area filled with vivid pictures and other intriguing children. There was a slight but real gap between them for the first time. Mehnaz waited in the school's waiting area, worrying that Anna may cry and miss her. However, it was the opposite of what she thought. Anna did not cry; after a few hours, her teacher came and asked Mehnaz if she could leave and come to pick her up once school is over. And she does not need to worry about Anna as she enjoys herself in class.

As she strolled back home, the breeze felt chillier, and the house was quieter than it had ever been. Mehnaz couldn't help but replay the morning in her mind—the joy, the smiles, and the slight pang of sorrow that came with letting go, even just a little.

It was the first day for everybody. For Anna, it was the start of new voyages, a world outside home protection. For her parents, it was the main step in seeing their baby grow, a sentimental remembrance of how quickly time moves.

And as Mehnaz sat down at the kitchen table, gazing at the small pair of shoes Anna had outgrown, she smiled. This was just the start of many magnificent, chaotic, and exceptional moments to come.

CHAPTER 8

THE BACKBONE OF LOVE

A mother's love is the type of anchor that remains unbroken, even in the deepest of hurricanes. She's the one who remains standing by you when the world feels like it's collapsing apart, her existence a token that you're certainly not truly abandoned.

For Mehnaz, this affection was the second characteristic. It was in the way she brought her child through their peaks and depths, never permitting her to feel the full weight of life's encounters. Whether it was a skinned knee from playing too harshly or a pain that left her child in tears, she was there—not with grand signs, but with a calm force that said, "I've got you."

Life wasn't always gentle to her, but she never let that dull her light. Even on days when she was struggling, her love never weakened. She was the constant beat in madness, the peace in her voice when everything else felt too noisy.

When her child faced her storms, Mehnaz was her refuge. She battled strongly to shield her from the world. Her love wasn't about flawlessness but about being there, no matter what.

And yet, she never asked for anything in return. She didn't require an ovation or acknowledgment.

Witnessing her kid smile, hearing her glee, or simply understanding she was safe was enough for her.

But a love like that shouldn't go unseen. Mothers like Mehnaz deserve more than just a simple "thank you." They are worthy of being seen, precious, and praised. Because through every hurricane, they are the ones who teach us how to stay strong, even when the winds are against us.

In every embrace, every believed prayer, and every sacrifice made in calm, there is a piece of love that only a mother can give. And for that, she deserves not just appreciation but a home in your heart that nothing else can replace.

A mother's love reflects the divine mercy surrounding us, a profound gift that even Allah SWT has emphasized its importance in the Quran. We are reminded of the duty to honor and care for our parents, to shower them with love and respect, especially as they age and grow more vulnerable.

Allah SWT, in His infinite wisdom, commands us to show kindness and compassion to our parents, especially in their later years. The Quran beautifully says:

"And We have enjoined upon man [care] for his parents. His mother carried him, [increasing her] in weakness upon weakness, and his weaning is in two years. Be grateful to

Me and to your parents; to Me is the [final] destination."
(Surah Luqman 31:14)

When they reach old age, we must protect their dignity, just as they protected us in childhood. We should lower our wings of humility and mercy, speak gently, and never show impatience. This is not just an act of love but worship, a way to draw closer to Allah SWT by fulfilling one of His greatest commandments.

Love and care for your parents, especially in their old age, is more than just a moral obligation; it is a divine duty. In doing so, we find blessings, peace, and the satisfaction of knowing that we have honored one of the greatest gifts Allah has given us: our parents.

CHAPTER 9

CHAPTERS YET TO COME

As this chapter concludes, the tale is far from over. Anna's once-free childhood from worry is now a memory she looks back on with yearning as she faces fears of growing up. Life feels tighter now, loaded with trials she wasn't ready for—moments of skepticism, battles to fit in, and the exploration for her place in a complex world.

But one factor stays constant: her mother's affection. Mehnaz, who then held Anna through sleepless nights and celebrated her slightest achievements, is still there, a quiet but continual presence. The lessons Anna learned from her mother—kindness, strength, and the courage to keep going—are now her compass, directing her through life's bends and turns.

This book isn't just an album of memoirs; it symbolizes the bonds that impact us and give us power. It's for anybody who's ever leaned on family in difficult times or received support knowing someone truly cares.

In a world where life often experiences dashed and relationships are taken for granted, this tale summons you to wait and reflect. It's an acknowledgment of the sacrifices parents make daily, frequently without appreciation, and the love that soundlessly clutches us amid difficult times.

At its fundamental, this story is about love, which is patient, enduring, and transformative. It's in the way parents offer their lives to their children, and how kids, in turn, learn to respect and value them. It's about the silent strength in showing up, compassion, and holding on, even when life feels devastating.

The story of Anna and Mehnaz doesn't finish here because life isn't a single period. It's an ever-developing journey packed with teachings, growth, and love. Their connection will continue to deepen as Anna steps into the world, led by the base her mother formed with untiring care.

This book is a call to witness beauty in the efforts, value the people who stay beside you, and hold the love that carries us through every storm. It's a story that reminds us that even when life feels uncertain, we are never truly alone.